KU-417-245

My First Pet

Rebecca Hunter

Photography by Chris Fairclough

Evans

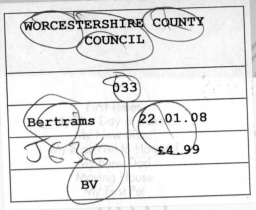

WORCESTERSHIRE COUNTY COUNCIL

033

Bertrams | 22.01.08

£4.99

BV

Published in paperback by Evans Brothers Ltd in 2006
2A Portman Mansions
Chiltern Street
London W1U 6NR
England

All rights reserved. No part of this publication may be reproduced, stored in a retrieval system, or transmitted in any form, or by any means, electronic, mechanical, photocopying, or otherwise, without prior permission of Evans Brothers Limited.

Hunter, Rebecca
My first pet. – (First Times)
1. Pets - Juvenile literature
I. Title
636'.0887

ISBN 0 237 53179 8
13-digit ISBN (from 1 Jan 2007) 978 0 237 53179 9

Acknowledgements

Planning and production by Discovery Books
Editor: Rebecca Hunter
Photographer: Chris Fairclough
Designer: Ian Winton
Consultant: Mark Stewart B.Vet. MED., M.R.C.V.S., is a practising veterinary surgeon in Shropshire.
The publishers would like to thank Rehaan Qureshi, Ayub Qureshi, Kim Healey and Bayley's Garden and Pet Centre, Shrewsbury for their help in the preparation of this book.
© Evans Brothers Limited 2000

VISIT OUR WEBSITE
Evans
www.evansbooks.co.uk

My First Pet

700031470339

My name is Rehaan.
This book tells you about
my first pet.

Contents

I would like a pet.

I have been saving my pocket money.

Dad says I have saved enough to buy a pet.

I am not sure what to get.

Dad and I look at some books about animals. I am not sure what sort of pet to get.

We go to the pet centre.

We go to the pet centre.
There are lots of animals
here to choose from.

I like the guinea pigs best.

There are fish
and birds and
rabbits and
hamsters.

I think I like the
guinea pigs best.

Here is a litter of guinea pigs.

Here is a litter of baby guinea pigs. They are six weeks old. I like the fluffy brown and white one.

I shall call her Daisy.

Kim, the assistant, gets her out and gives her to me to hold. She is really sweet. I would like to buy her. I shall call her Daisy.

We buy a cage.

Kim tells us what we will need.

We buy a cage and some hay and sawdust. We also need some food and a bowl and a water bottle.

We take Daisy home.

Kim puts all the things inside the cage and puts Daisy in a box.

We take Daisy home.

I get the cage ready.

When we get
home I get
the cage
ready. First
I put in the sawdust, then I put
in some hay.

I put Daisy
gently into
her new
cage.

Daisy loves carrots!

I fill up her water
bottle and give
her some food.

She really loves
the carrot!

I feed Daisy every morning.

I feed Daisy every morning.
She has special guinea pig food.
It is important not to give
her too much.

She loves
fresh fruit and
vegetables too.

I clean out her cage.

Once a week I clean out her cage. I throw away the old sawdust and hay.

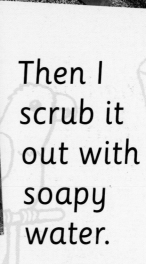

Then I scrub it out with soapy water.

Daisy has an outside run.

We have built an outside run for Daisy. When it is fine weather, she can go outside. She loves running around on the grass.

I love my guinea pig.

Sometimes I let her out to play with me. She doesn't run away because she knows me now.

I love my guinea pig.

Index

Notes on keeping pets

About guinea pigs

The guinea pig is more accurately called a cavy and is originally from South America.

Guinea pigs are born well developed and are ready to leave their mother between three and four weeks old.

Either sex make good pets. If a non-breeding pair is wanted, two females are more advisable since they are less likely to fight.

Guinea pigs should be kept in a well-ventilated cage in a dry, draught-free area. They can be kept outside in summer but their cage should be brought indoors in winter.

Guinea pigs should be fed on a proprietary brand guinea pig food. Rabbit food is **not** suitable. They will also enjoy fresh vegetables and some fruits, but these should be fed sparingly as too much will cause diarrhoea.

A fresh supply of water should always be available.

Guinea pigs are hardy animals and if looked after well should remain healthy over their lifespan of four to five years.

Advice from the vet

- Never buy a pet on impulse. Keeping a pet involves years of commitment and should not be undertaken lightly.

- Take time to consider what sort of pet will be suitable in your circumstances. Think about: the size and location of your house, the time you have available for looking after a pet, the cost of buying your pet, its equipment and food.

- If the pet is to belong to a child, make sure he or she understands the responsibility and work involved in owning a pet.

- Buy your pet from a reputable breeder or pet centre.

- Choose a bright-eyed, clean-coated healthy-looking animal. If in any doubt, get a vet to examine the animal before taking it home.

- Buy a good reference book about the type of pet you choose. This should give you all the necessary information you will need on how to look after it as well as how to get the most enjoyment from keeping your pet.

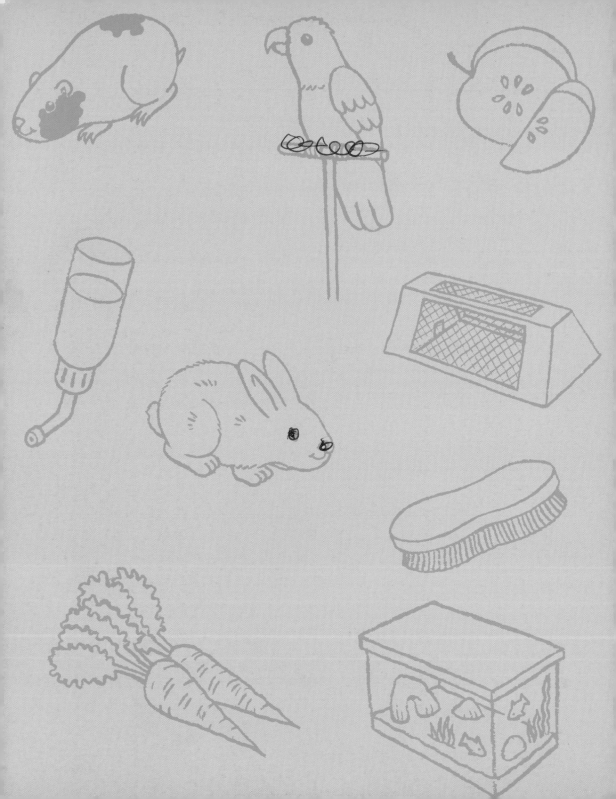